EXTREME SKIING

Weigl Publishers Inc.

Published by Weigl Publishers Inc.
350 5th Avenue, Suite 3304, PMB 6G
New York, NY 10118-0069

Website: www.weigl.com

All of the Internet URLs given in the book were valid at the time of publication. However,
due to the dynamic nature of the Internet, some addresses may have changed, or sites
may have ceased to exist since publication. While the author and publisher regret any
inconvenience this may cause readers, no responsibility for any such changes can be
accepted by either the author or the publisher.

Library of Congress Cataloging-in-Publication Data available upon request.
Fax 1-866-44-WEIGL for the attention of the Publishing Records department.

ISBN 978-1-59036-918-0 (hard cover)
ISBN 978-1-59036-919-7 (soft cover)

Printed in the United States of America
1 2 3 4 5 6 7 8 9 0   12 11 10 09 08

Weigl would like to acknowledge Getty Images as its primary photo supplier for this title.

Every reasonable effort has been made to trace ownership and to obtain permission
to reprint copyright material. The publishers would be pleased to have any errors
or omissions brought to their attention so that they may be corrected in
subsequent printings.

EDITOR: Heather C. Hudak
DESIGN: Terry Paulhus
LAYOUT: Kathryn Livingstone

EXTREME SKIING

CONTENTS

WHAT ARE THE X GAMES?

The X Games are an annual sports tournament that showcases the best athletes in the extreme sports world. Extreme sports are performed at high speeds. Participants must wear special equipment to help protect them from injury. Only athletes who spend years training should take part in these sports. There are many competitions, such as the X Games, that celebrate the skill, dedication, and determination of the athletes, as well as the challenge and difficulty of the sports.

The X Games began as the Extreme Games in 1995. The following year, the name was shortened to X Games. In 1995 and 1996, the games were held in the summer, and they featured a wide variety of sports. These included skateboarding, inline skating, BMX, street luge, sky surfing, and rock climbing.

The popularity of the X Games made it possible for more sports to be showcased. In 1997, the Winter X Games began. The Winter X Games feature sports such as snowboarding, skiing, and snowmobiling. Today, there are Summer and Winter X Games each year.

Some of the best skiers in the world compete in the X Games. These athletes perform extreme moves in front of large crowds. Events feature skies flying through the air or racing at high speeds.

TECHNOLINK

Learn more about the X Games at **expn.go.com**.

X FEST

The X Games are about more than sports. Each year, musical acts from all over the world perform for fans at the X Games. X Fest is the name for the musical portion of the X Games. It features some of the best-known punk rock, hip hop, and alternative music artists of the time. These artists perform between sporting events and keep the crowds entertained and excited for the competitions.

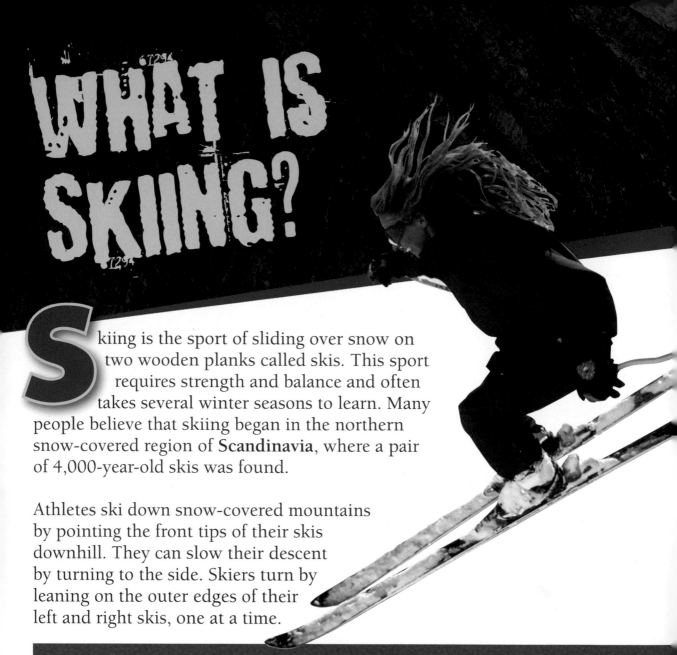

WHAT IS SKIING?

Skiing is the sport of sliding over snow on two wooden planks called skis. This sport requires strength and balance and often takes several winter seasons to learn. Many people believe that skiing began in the northern snow-covered region of **Scandinavia**, where a pair of 4,000-year-old skis was found.

Athletes ski down snow-covered mountains by pointing the front tips of their skis downhill. They can slow their descent by turning to the side. Skiers turn by leaning on the outer edges of their left and right skis, one at a time.

Timeline

2000 BC – People in Scandinavia use skis as a way of crossing large distances.

1890 – The word "ski" enters the English language from the Norwegian language.

1904 – The National Ski Association is founded in Michigan.

1924 – The *Fédération Internationale de Ski* is created, and skiing becomes part of the first Winter Olympics.

1930s – Freestyle skiing begins when cross-country alpine skiers start to perform tricks.

1988 – Freestyle skiing is showcased at the Olympics in Calgary, Canada.

To stop, skiers must make a sharp left or right turn. Both of their skis will point to the side of the hill rather than downhill. This method is very similar to how ice skaters and hockey players stop while on the ice. It is often referred to as a hockey stop. Skiers also can stop by pointing the skis together at the front, forming a V shape with the planks.

Today, there are many kinds of skiing. Two main types are Nordic and Alpine skiing. Nordic skiing is done on flat trails. People glide along, using the skis to cut through the snow. Alpine skiing is often called downhill skiing. It was developed in the Alps mountain range, which stretches across the European countries of France, Italy, Slovenia, Switzerland, Germany, and Austria. The X Games showcases downhill skiers that use **kickers** and rails to perform jumps, flips, twists, and other feats. This extreme form of skiing is often called freestyle skiing. It can be a very dangerous sport. Skiers take many safety precautions and keep themselves in peak physical shape to perform stunts.

Skiers can carry their equipment to natural trails in mountains and forests.

1990s – Freestyle skiers start performing tricks at snowboard parks—taking the sport to a new level.

1998 – Skiing becomes part of the X Games.

2003 – The X Games holds a special event called the Global Championships, where six continents compete in a series of winter and summer X Games sports. Ski competitions are held in Whistler, British Columbia, Canada.

2008 – For the first time, audience members can vote for the winner of the X Games Big Air Ski competition by texting their choice with their cell phones.

ALL THE RIGHT EQUIPMENT

At one time, people living in snowy places used skis as their main means of travel over long distances. They used ski equipment that was quite different from the gear that is used for downhill skiing today. For instance, skiers wore flexible boots that only attached the toe of the ski, leaving the heel free. The movement of the heel made it possible to push the skis along flat terrain with the help of poles. Today, skiers wear special **rigid** boots that attach to binding on their skis. The boots prevent skiers' feet and ankles from moving.

Since skiing is a winter sport, it requires warm, water-resistant clothing. Many skiers wear thermal shirts and pants under a well-insulated ski jacket and snow pants. Ski socks are important because skiers' feet cannot move in ski boots. The lack of movement decreases blood flow, and feet can get very cold. To prevent frostbite, skiers must wear special ski or winter socks, often made of wool, to protect their feet. A hat and gloves are also important.

ACCESSORIZE IT !

Goggles protect skiers' eyes from sunlight, snow, and wind. They have a plastic or rubber frame with foam padding that fits snugly on the face, so no air gets inside. Goggles have different colors of lenses for various conditions. Yellow lenses are good for most conditions. They can be used in low to moderate light. Goggles have a wide elastic band that fits around the back of a skier's head or helmet.

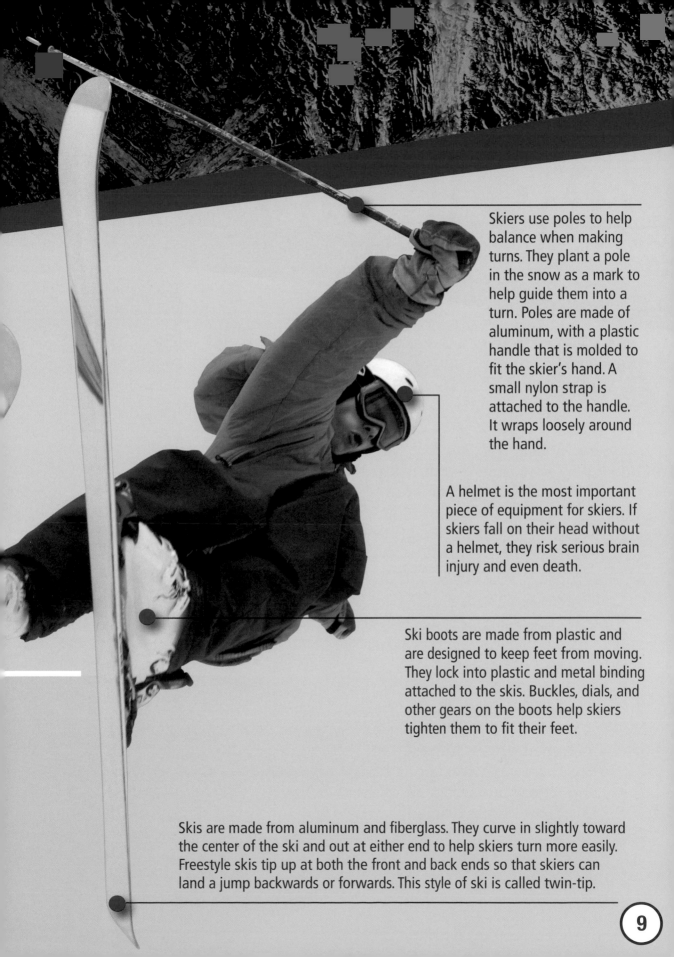

Skiers use poles to help balance when making turns. They plant a pole in the snow as a mark to help guide them into a turn. Poles are made of aluminum, with a plastic handle that is molded to fit the skier's hand. A small nylon strap is attached to the handle. It wraps loosely around the hand.

A helmet is the most important piece of equipment for skiers. If skiers fall on their head without a helmet, they risk serious brain injury and even death.

Ski boots are made from plastic and are designed to keep feet from moving. They lock into plastic and metal binding attached to the skis. Buckles, dials, and other gears on the boots help skiers tighten them to fit their feet.

Skis are made from aluminum and fiberglass. They curve in slightly toward the center of the ski and out at either end to help skiers turn more easily. Freestyle skis tip up at both the front and back ends so that skiers can land a jump backwards or forwards. This style of ski is called twin-tip.

SURVEYING THE VENUE

Most skiing takes places at ski hills or resorts in mountain ranges. Ski hills are built where there are steep trails. Trees are cut down to form runs. Lifts, including **gondolas**, chair lifts, **rope tows** and **t-bars**, take skiers and snowboarders to the tops of different runs. Runs are marked by name and difficulty level. A green circle means the run is for beginners. A blue square stands for intermediate, and a black diamond is for advanced skiers only. A double black diamond is extremely difficult and for expert skiers. These difficulty levels are all based on the skill needed to ski a certain hill. All green runs will not be at the exact same level of difficulty on every hill around the world. In addition to different types of runs, many ski hills have special parks with rails, kickers, and **halfpipes** to help perform jumps and tricks.

In the X Games, both hills and parks are used for skiing events. In Skier X and **Slopestyle**, riders race down groomed runs, similar to those found on ski hills. However, these runs also have a number of park features, such as rails and tabletop jumps. These jumps have ramps up the front and back, with a flat area at the top. For Superpipe and Big Air events, skiers perform stunts as they ride along a halfpipe or fly through the air.

Ski parks often have rails to ride.

TECHNOLINK

To check out the venue for the winter X-Games from 2002-2010 at Buttermilk Mountain in Aspen, Colorado, visit **www.aspensnowmass.com /buttermilk/default.cfm**.

BIG AIR

The Big Air X Games event began as a snowboarding competition, but in 1999, a ski event was added. Since then, Big Air has become one of the most popular events. It features four of the world's top skiers battling for first place.

In the Big Air event, skiers launch off a ramp, performing aerial stunts as they soar through the air. Competitors are judged on their best trick. Each skier gets two runs, performing exciting tricks each time. He must try to land the tricks solidly. Top points are given to competitors who land facing backward.

Boyd Easley has taken part in many X Games competitions.

During the 2008 Big Air competition, both judges and fans were allowed to vote for the winner for the first time in X Games history. Half of the score was based on the official judges' scores. The other half of the score was left to fans who could vote online at expn.com or by texting their choice on their cell phones. Fans watching the game live on TV and at the site were allowed to vote.

All X Games ski judges are former professional skiers and X Games competitors.

BIG AIR PAST WINNERS

2008
Gold – Torstein Horgmo
Silver – Kevin Pearce
Bronze – Travis Rice and Andreas Wiig

SUPERPIPE

In 2002, the Superpipe competition was added to the X Games. This event features a 500-foot (152-meter) long, 17-foot-deep, u-shaped pipe that is 54 feet (16 m) from edge to edge with a slope of 16 degrees. The huge pipe allows skiers to gain speed and air so that they can perform bigger and more exciting tricks.

Skiers competing in Superpipe are judged on the difficulty of the tricks they perform while skiing down the pipe. These tricks are limited only by skiers' imagination and ability. Skiers use the downward slope of the hill to gain speed. As they ski down the pipe, they shoot up both sides and into the air to perform spins, sommersaults, and turns.

The men's Superpipe competition has two rounds. In the first round, each skier takes two runs and is ranked based on his best score of the two. The top 10 skiers continue to the final round. In the finals, each skier takes three runs. The skier with the best score out of the three final runs wins gold.

Jon Olsson has won eight Winter X Games medals.

The women's competition has one round. Ten athletes take two runs each. The skiers are ranked on the best score of their two runs. The woman with the highest score wins.

Ski and snowboard superpipes and halfpipes are made from snow that has been tightly packed.

SUPERPIPE PAST WINNERS

2008
Men's Gold – Tanner Hall
Men's Silver – Simon Dumont
Men's Bronze – Colby West

Women's Gold – Sarah Burke
Women's Silver – Mirjam Jaeger
Women's Bronze – Jen Hudak

SKIER X

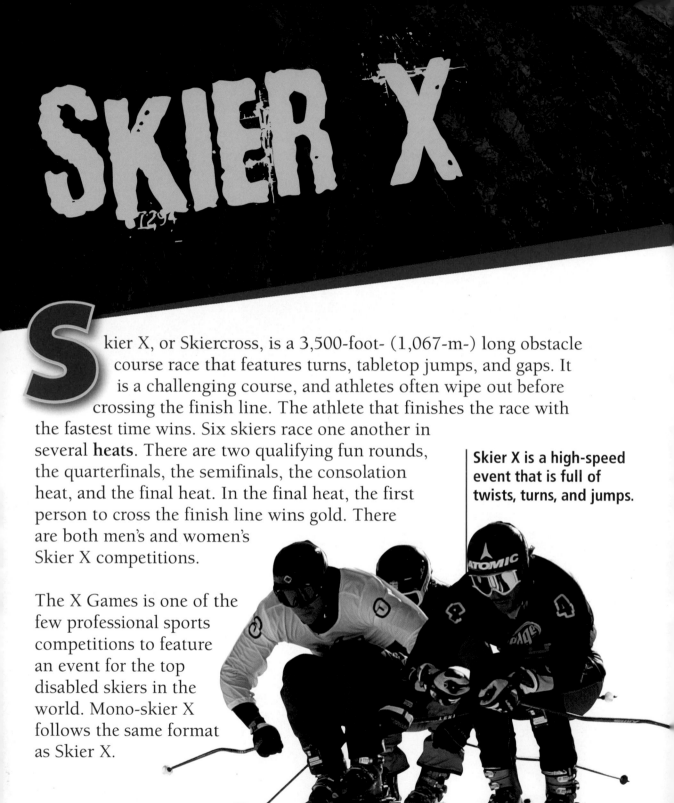

Skier X, or Skiercross, is a 3,500-foot- (1,067-m-) long obstacle course race that features turns, tabletop jumps, and gaps. It is a challenging course, and athletes often wipe out before crossing the finish line. The athlete that finishes the race with the fastest time wins. Six skiers race one another in several **heats**. There are two qualifying fun rounds, the quarterfinals, the semifinals, the consolation heat, and the final heat. In the final heat, the first person to cross the finish line wins gold. There are both men's and women's Skier X competitions.

Skier X is a high-speed event that is full of twists, turns, and jumps.

The X Games is one of the few professional sports competitions to feature an event for the top disabled skiers in the world. Mono-skier X follows the same format as Skier X.

Mono-skiers use a specially designed single ski with a seat. They use two poles with runners on the bottom to help balance themselves while turning.

Mono-skier X debuted in 2005 as a demonstration event. It became a medaled event in 2007. It is now a permanent competition at the Winter X Games.

SKIER X PAST WINNERS

2008

Men's Gold – Daron Rahlves
Men's Silver – Stanley Hayer
Men's Bronze – Casey Puckett

Women's Gold – Ophelie David
Women's Silver – Hedda Bernsten
Women's Bronze – Magdalena Jonsson

Mono-skier Gold – Kees-Jan van der Klooster
Mono-skier Silver – Tyler Walker
Mono-skier Bronze – Chris Devlin-Young

QUALIFYING TO COMPETE

The first step to becoming a professional skier is to be sponsored. Companies sponsor skiers by paying them to wear their brand name or logo at competitions. Sometimes, the skier appears in TV and magazine advertisements selling the sponsor company's product. Soft drink companies and sports manufacturers are examples of companies that sponsor athletes. Although X Games competitors do not need a sponsor to qualify for the games, they do need money to pay for the latest sports equipment, travel to competitions around the world, and pay for living expenses while practicing skiing. To become sponsored, a person must be very good at skiing.

TECHNOLINK

To learn more about getting sponsored, check out **www.volantski.com**, **www.rossignol.com**, and **www2.head.com/ski/region.php**.

Sometimes, companies will approach athletes about sponsorship. However, most companies will not know about a good skier unless that person is competing at big events. For this reason, many skiers contact companies about sponsorship. Most ski equipment companies have information about sponsorship on their websites.

To qualify for the X Games, a skier must compete in other ski events throughout the year, including World Cup competitions. The top skiers in each competition qualify for the X Games.

Beginner skiers can join a professional skiing tour or organization to gain entrance into the X Games. National tours often have some of the same sponsors as the Winter X Games. Top performing skiers on these tours may qualify for upcoming X Games. Beginners are able to participate in ski exhibitions and demonstrations to show their skills. Winter X Games organizers often go to these events and may be able to help talented beginners get into the X Games.

People interested in competing in the X Games for the first time can read local ski magazines and websites to learn about qualifying events in their areas. Winter X Games organizers look at the results of many ski competitions throughout the United States to find competitors.

SIMILAR SPORTS

While skiing is a unique sport that is popular around the world, there are many other sports that use skis or a board on snow. These sports are similar to skiing.

Ski Jumping

In ski jumping, skiers go down a special run that has a take-off ramp at the end. The goal is to travel or jump as far as possible. Ski jumping is a competitive sport and part of the Winter Olympic Games. Skiers are judged on the length of their jump and their style, or form. Ski jumpers have special boots that do not attach to their skis at the heel. This allows the jumpers to lean forward in a more **aerodynamic** shape so that they can jump farther.

Waterskiing

In waterskiing, a person holds onto a rope that is attached to a motorboat. As the boat moves, the person is dragged across a still body of water. Waterskiers stay on top of the water because of surface tension and the high speed at which the boat is moving. Waterskiers often use floating ramps in the water to jump into the air. They can perform tricks, such as flips or huge jumps.

Snowboarding

Snowboarding is a mix of surfing and skiing. Boarders ride a wide, flat board down a snow-covered hill. Snowboarders wear flexible boots, and their feet are strapped onto the board.

Ski BASE

Ski base, or ski BASE jumping, is a fairly new sport. It is based on the extreme and highly dangerous sport of BASE jumping in which people jump off tall objects, such as buildings. In ski BASE, people ski off cliffs, performing sommersaults and other tricks in the air, before releasing a parachute on their back to take them safely to the ground.

UNFORGETTABLE MOMENTS

The X Games has had many unforgettable moments. These include breath-taking stunts, record-breaking wins, and cringe-worthy wipeouts.

The 2008 Skier X course had some of the worst crashes in X Games history. Most of the spills happened at the second-to-last jump on the course. To begin, Enak Gavaggio of France and Lars Lewen of Sweden crashed during the quarterfinals. Both men came off the jump leaning too far back and fell to the ground. Juha Haukkala of Finland caught a ski on the hand of another skier on the same jump and was knocked down. Austrian Karin Huttary, Merryl Boulangeat of France, and Slovenian Sasa Faric crashed on the same jump.

During X Games 11, Hiroomi Takizawa of Japan was carried away by medical aids after a crash in the Skier X event.

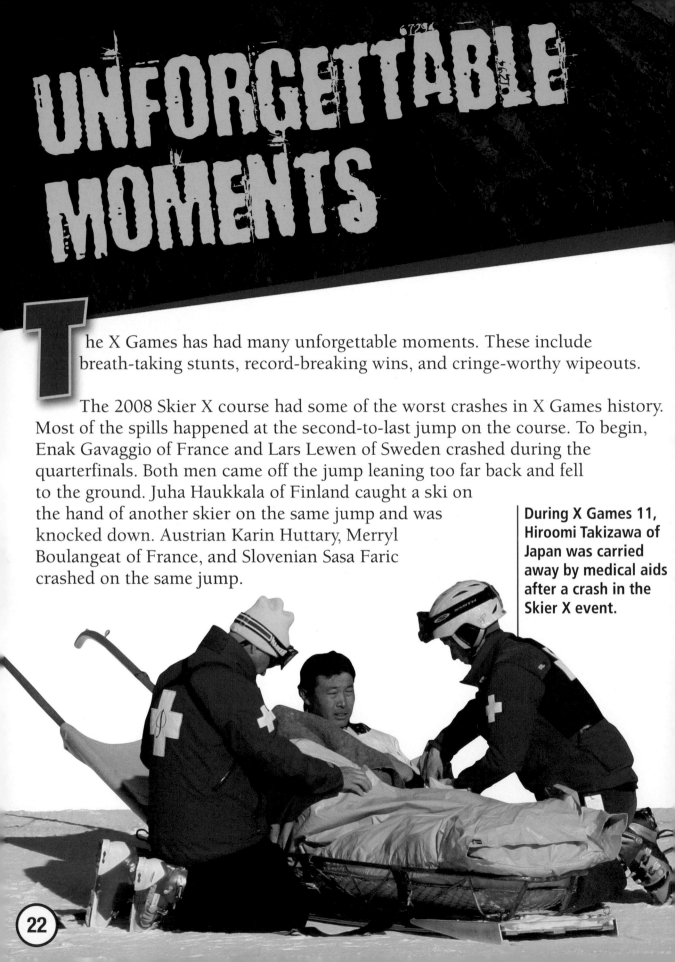

Known as the Flying Dutchman, Kees-Jan van der Klooster from Holland is a mono-skier. In 2007, Kees-Jan, or K. J., won the X Games bronze medal, and Tyler Walker went home with the gold. Although favored to win the gold again in 2008, Tyler took silver after two other competitors wiped out. K.J. landed an 85-foot (26-m) kicker, or jump, at the end of the course, gaining a major advantage and winning the gold. Sports commentators called the race one of the most exciting events to watch at the X Games.

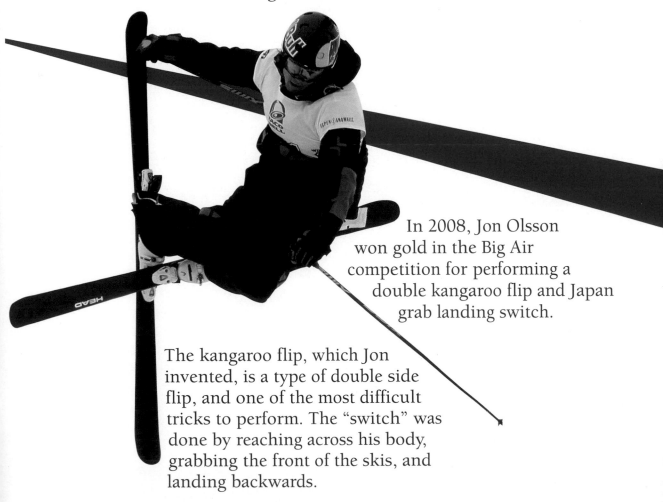

In 2008, Jon Olsson won gold in the Big Air competition for performing a double kangaroo flip and Japan grab landing switch.

The kangaroo flip, which Jon invented, is a type of double side flip, and one of the most difficult tricks to perform. The "switch" was done by reaching across his body, grabbing the front of the skis, and landing backwards.

AROUND THE WORLD

Whistler Blackcomb, Canada

Whistler Blackcomb is Canada's largest ski area. Located in the Fitzsimmons Range, it was the site of the X Games Global Championships in 2003. The hill has 8,100 acres (3,278 hectares), more than 200 runs, 3 glaciers, and 38 lifts.

ATLANTIC OCEAN

Sunshine Village, Canada

Sunshine Village is 7,000 feet (2,134 m) above the valley below and can only be reached by a high-speed gondola that ferries people up the hill. The resort is known for having a great deal of natural snow. Sunshine is open from mid-November until late May. It has a longer season than most ski hills.

Aspen, United States

Aspen, a ski resort in Colorado, has been the home of the Winter X Games since 2002. Aspen has four mountains, which feature a variety of runs for every level of skier. Buttermilk Mountain, the site of the 2008 X Games, has wide open, gentle slopes that are perfect for beginners and for building race courses and the superpipe.

Games Venues

1. Whistler, Canada
2. Aspen, United States
3. Big Bear Lake, United States
4. Crested Butte, United States
5. Mount Snow, United States

ARCTIC OCEAN

ARCTIC OCEAN

Niseko Hirafu, Japan

Located in snow-covered Hokkaido, Niseko Hirafu is one of Japan's top resorts for **powder** skiing. The area gets warm weather fronts, or air that travels across the sea, from the Siberian desert. While on the mountain, skiers can view the volcano Mt. Yotei, as well as the Sea of Japan.

Alpe d'Huez, France

Alpe d'Huez is located in the French Alps. Alpe d'Huez has long hours of sunshine. Its name means "the island in the Sun." The resort is so large that people can ski for nearly one-and-a-half hours without using ski lifts. The Sarenne run is the longest run in the world, at 10 miles (16 km).

PACIFIC OCEAN

INDIAN OCEAN

Perisher Blue, Australia

Perisher Blue is one of Australia's largest ski resorts. It has 3,076 acres (1,245 hectares) of runs spread over seven peaks. Freestyle skiers can check out the four terrain parks and two halfpipes. Perisher Blue is host to the Australian Winter X Games.

CURRENT STARS

SARAH BURKE

HOMETOWN
Whistler, British
Columbia, Canada

BORN
September 3, 1982

NOTES
Was awarded the Best
Female Action Sports Athlete
ESPY & BERT Award in 2007

Is the first skier to win an
ESPY award

Won gold for performing a **900**
or two-and-a-half spins, during the
2008 Superpipe event

Performed stunts in several ski
movies, including *Propaganda*

JON OLSSON

HOMETOWN
Mora, Sweden

BORN
August 17, 1982

NOTES
Has tied the record with Tanner
Hall for most Winter X Games
medals, at 10

Decided to train for Olympic ski
racing in 2008

The oldest competitor
competing in both
slopestyle and Big Air

TANNER HALL

HOMETOWN
Kalispell, Montana,
United States

BORN
October 26, 1983

NOTES
Tied for the most gold
medals of any athlete at
the Winter X Games—seven

Fractured both heels and ankle
bones in a ski accident in 2005

Has won at least one medal every
year that he has competed in the
X Games

GRETE ELIASSEN

HOMETOWN
Lillehammer, Norway

BORN
September 19, 1986

NOTES
Won gold at the first
women's Superpipe medal
event at 18 years old

Won gold in the 2005 X Games even
though she accidentally landed her
last trick with her legs still crossed

LEGENDS

SHANE McCONKEY

HOMETOWN
Vancouver, British
Columbia, Canada

BORN
December 30, 1969

NOTES
Was born to a family
of skiers—his mom competes
in the sport, and his dad ran
a ski school

A professional ski BASE jumper
who did a double front flip off
Eiger Mountain

Fell in love with ski BASE
jumping while watching
James Bond ski off a
cliff and open his
parachute in the
opening scene of The
Spy Who Loved Me

LLOYD LANGLOIS

HOMETOWN
Magog, Quebec, Canada

BORN
November 11, 1962

NOTES
Won gold and silver medals
47 times at the World Cup
for ski aerials

Competed as a freestyle
skier for 13 years

DONNA WEINBRECHT

HOMETOWN
Hoboken, New Jersey,
United States

BORN
April 23, 1965

NOTES
Started skiing when she
was seven years old

With a friend, started a ski team
at her high school

Was a top **mogul** skier known
as "the bump queen of the
United States"

CHRIS ERNST

HOMETOWN
Tahoe, Nevada,
United States

NOTES
Nicknamed Uncle E

Created a festival for
skiers, snowboarders, and
telemarkers called Lord
of the Boards

THE 10 QUESTION QUIZ

1. Who invented the kangaroo flip?

2. What year did Sarah Burke win t[he] gold medal in Superpipe?

3. What is the most important piece of safety equipment skiers use?

4. When did the first winter X Game[s] take place?

5. What is ski BASE?

6. How old is skiing?

7. When was skiing introduced to the X Games?

8. Who landed her last trick incorrect[ly] but still won gold?

9. What are three X Games ski events[?]

10. What is X Fest?

Answers: 1. Jon Olsson 2. 2008 3. a helmet [4.] 1997 5. skiing off a cliff, performing a trick, and then releasing a parachute attached to the [s]kier's back 6. more than 4,000 years old [7.] 1997 8. Grete Eliassen 9. Big Air, Superpipe, [a]nd Skier X 10. a music festival at the X Games

RESEARCH

www.expn.go.com

www.aspensnowmass.com

www.abc-of-skiing.com

www.planetx.com.au

Many books and websites provide information on skiing. To learn more, borrow books from the library, or surf the Internet.

Most libraries have computers that connect to a database for researching information. If you input a keyword, you will be provided with a list of books in the library that contain information on that topic. Non-fiction books are arranged numerically, using their call number. Fiction books are organized alphabetically by the author's last name

900: two-and-a-half spins in the air

aerodynamic: designed with rounded edges to reduce wind drag and increase speed

gondolas: cabins on a lift that is used to carry people to the top of a mountain

halfpipes: two ramps that curve inward and are facing each other with an area of flat ground between them

heats: races in which competitors attempt to qualify for entry in the final race

kickers: ski jumps used to perform tricks

mogul: a series of consistent bumps or small hills on a ski run

powder: deep, fluffy snow

rigid: not flexible

rope tows: ropes that pull people to the top of a hill

Scandinavia: a region that includes Denmark, Norway, Sweden, and sometimes Iceland, Finland, and the Faroe Islands

Slopestyle: a type of skiing that has skiers selecting a path through a series of obstacles

t-bars: bars that look like an upside-down "T" that skiers can lean on while being towed uphill

telemarkers: downhill skiers that use special skis with detached heels; they bend their knee on their turning side at a 90-degree angle while pushing back with the opposite leg